Get to Know Inclined Planes

by Jennifer Christiansen

Crabtree Publishing Company

www.crabtreebooks.com

Crabtree Publishing Company

www.crabtreebooks.com

Author: Jennifer Christiansen
Editors: Molly Aloian, Reagan Miller, Crystal Sikkens
Project coordinator: Robert Walker
Prepress technicians: Ken Wright, Margaret Amy Salter
Production coordinator: Margaret Amy Salter
Cover design: Samara Parent
Coordinating editor: Chester Fisher
Series and project editor: Penny Dowdy
Project manager: Kumar Kunal (Q2AMEDIA)
Art direction: Dibakar Acharjee (Q2AMEDIA)
Design: Ritu Chopra (Q2AMEDIA)
Photo research: Farheen Aadil (Q2AMEDIA)

Illustrations:
Q2AMedia Art Bank: p. 8, 9, 12, 13, 16, 17, 20, 21, 24, 25, 28, 29

Photographs:
Alamy: Lee Foster: p. 10
Corbis: Lowell Georgia: p. 14 (bottom left); Owen Franken: p. 22 (top)
Ingram photo objects: p. 4 (lever)
Istockphoto: Clayton Hansen: p. 4 (wheel and axle); Grant Shimmin: p. 7; Sally Scott: p. 22 (bottom); Alexey Stiop: p. 26
Jupiterimages: p. 6; Peter & Georgina Bowater: p. 14 (top right); Barrie Rokeach: p. 15
John Cancalosi/Photolibrary: p. 23
Shutterstock: nra: cover; Medvedev Andrey: p. 4 (screw); Andrjuss: p. 4 (wedge); Julián Rovagnati: p. 4 (inclined plane), 31; Harley Molesworth: p. 4 (pulley); Juriah Mosin: p. 5; Jarno Gonzalez Zarraonandia: p. 11; Margaret Smeaton: p. 18; Elena Elisseeva: p. 19; John Leung: p. 27

Library and Archives Canada Cataloguing in Publication

Christiansen, Jennifer
    Get to know inclined planes / Jennifer Christiansen.

(Get to know simple machines)
Includes index.
ISBN 978-0-7787-4466-5 (bound).--ISBN 978-0-7787-4483-2 (pbk.)

    1. Inclined planes--Juvenile literature.
I. Title. II. Series: Get to know simple machines

TJ147.C47 2009   j621.8   C2009-900726-6

Library of Congress Cataloging-in-Publication Data

Christiansen, Jennifer.
    Get to know inclined planes / Jennifer Christiansen.
        p. cm. -- (Get to know simple machines)
    Includes index.
    ISBN 978-0-7787-4483-2 (pbk. : alk. paper) -- ISBN 978-0-7787-4466-5 (reinforced library binding : alk. paper)
    1. Inclined planes--Juvenile literature. I. Title. II. Series.

TJ147.C534 2009
621.8--dc22

                                        2009003874

Crabtree Publishing Company

www.crabtreebooks.com   1-800-387-7650

Printed in the U.S.A./022015/CG20150122

Published in Canada
Crabtree Publishing
616 Welland Ave.
St. Catharines, ON
L2M 5V6

Published in the United States
Crabtree Publishing
PMB 59051
350 Fifth Avenue, 59th Floor
New York, New York 10118

Published in the United Kingdom
Crabtree Publishing
Maritime House
Basin Road North, Hove
BN41 1WR

Published in Australia
Crabtree Publishing
3 Charles Street
Coburg North
VIC, 3058

Contents

What is a Simple Machine?

All people have jobs to do. Some jobs take a lot of **energy**. Energy is the ability to do work. Simple machines help people get jobs done without working too hard. This is called **mechanical advantage**.

Simple machines are tools that are made up of very few parts. There are six kinds of simple machines. They are inclined planes, levers, pulleys, wedges, screws, and wheels and axles.

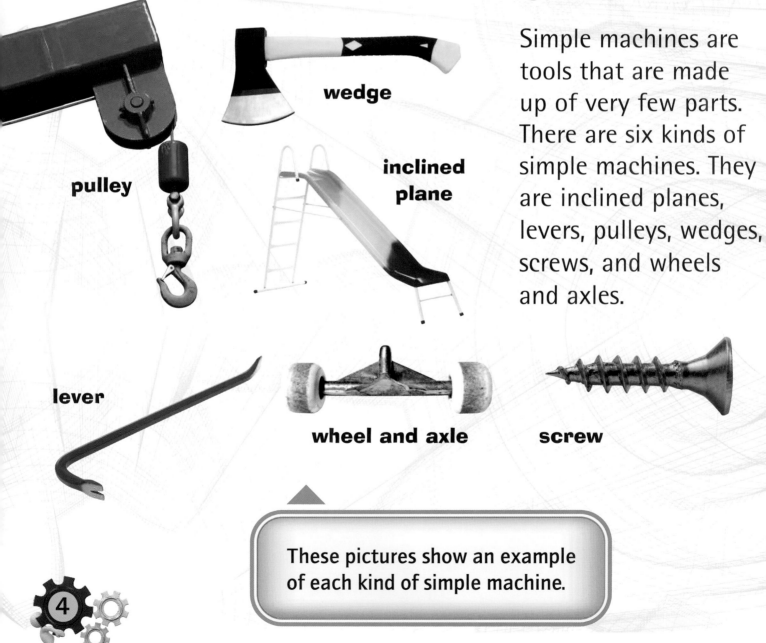

pulley

wedge

inclined plane

lever

wheel and axle

screw

These pictures show an example of each kind of simple machine.

One kind of simple machine is an **inclined plane**. Inclined planes are built on an **angle**. Inclined planes help us raise things up or bring things down without using much energy.

Whee! Have you ever slid down a slide? A slide is an inclined plane. Ramps and staircases are other examples of inclined planes found around us.

Ramp it Up!

A ramp is an inclined plane. Ramps are flat surfaces raised at an angle or incline. Ramps make work easier. It is easier to push a wagon up a ramp than to pick the wagon up.

A **force** is a push or pull that causes an object to move, change direction, or stop. You use force to push a box up a ramp. It takes less force to push the box down the ramp.

This ramp makes it easy to load and unload boxes.

A ramp may have **friction**. Friction is the force of one object rubbing against another. Friction causes objects to slow down. Imagine trying to ride a bike down a gravel hill. The force of the gravel rubbing against your bike's tires slows you down.

Build a Ramp

Now try making a ramp for yourself! You will need:

blanket or towel

paper

pencil

books

toy car

measuring tape

First, place the book on the floor. What happens when you set the car on the book? Is there something you can do to make the car move? That's right, make a ramp!

Tilt the book up about one inch (2.5 cm) and the car will roll. Measure the distance the car traveled from the bottom of the ramp to where the car stopped. Write down the distance.

Tilt the ramp up about three inches (7.6 cm). How far did the car travel this time? Measure and write it down. This time, raise the ramp six inches (15.2 cm). Why does the car keep traveling farther?

Now try adding friction. Perform the same experiment above, but place a blanket or towel over the book. Are the effects the same when you added friction? Why or why not?

Staircase

Another useful inclined plane is a staircase. A staircase helps you get to high places using less **effort**. The height of a staircase is called the **rise**. The problem with stairs is that you have to climb a longer distance to get to where you want to go. This is because stairs are built on an angle to make the distance you have to go less **steep**. You will use less energy if steps are built close together than if they are far away from each other. Stairs are used all over your neighborhood to make it easy for you to get around.

Queen Victoria ruled for 65 years. The same number of stairs are in this staircase built in her honor.

There are over 100 flights of steps in this old city. The steps help travelers explore with less effort.

Machu Picchu in Peru was built by the Incas around 1460. These early people made staircases to help them travel easily around their mountainside city.

What's the Advantage?

Find out how different staircases use different amounts of your energy to climb.

Both of these staircases are the same height.

A

B

Staircase A has four stairs. The stairs are far apart. You would need to take big steps to climb this staircase. It would take a lot of energy.

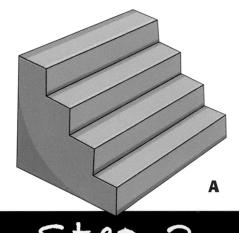

A

Step 1

Step 2

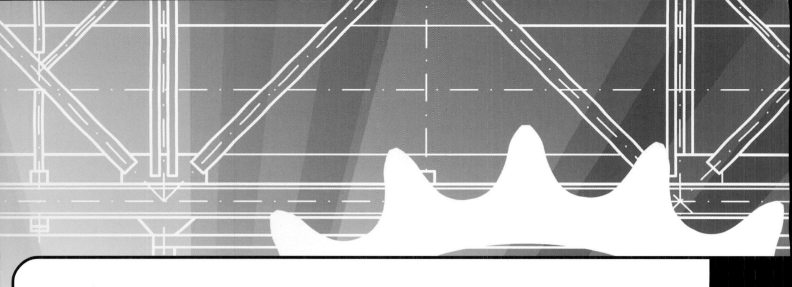

Staircase B has seven stairs. The stairs are closer together than the stairs of staircase A. You would need to take small steps to reach the top of staircase B.

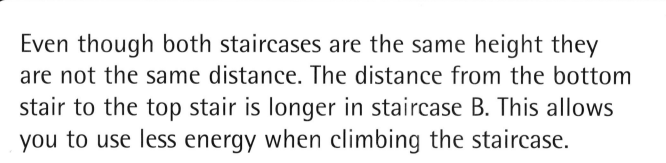

B

Even though both staircases are the same height they are not the same distance. The distance from the bottom stair to the top stair is longer in staircase B. This allows you to use less energy when climbing the staircase.

longer distance = less energy
shorter distance = more energy

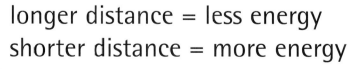

A   **B**

13

Trails and Roads

Trails and roads are inclined planes used by many people. They often have a zig-zag pattern called a **switchback**.

Why walk through the tall grass? Even some animals use and make trails to make traveling easier.

Imagine trying to walk straight up this mountain! The zig-zag trail helps hikers use less energy on their climb.

Switchbacks help people, cars, and animals use less energy to climb. The long, winding path is less steep.

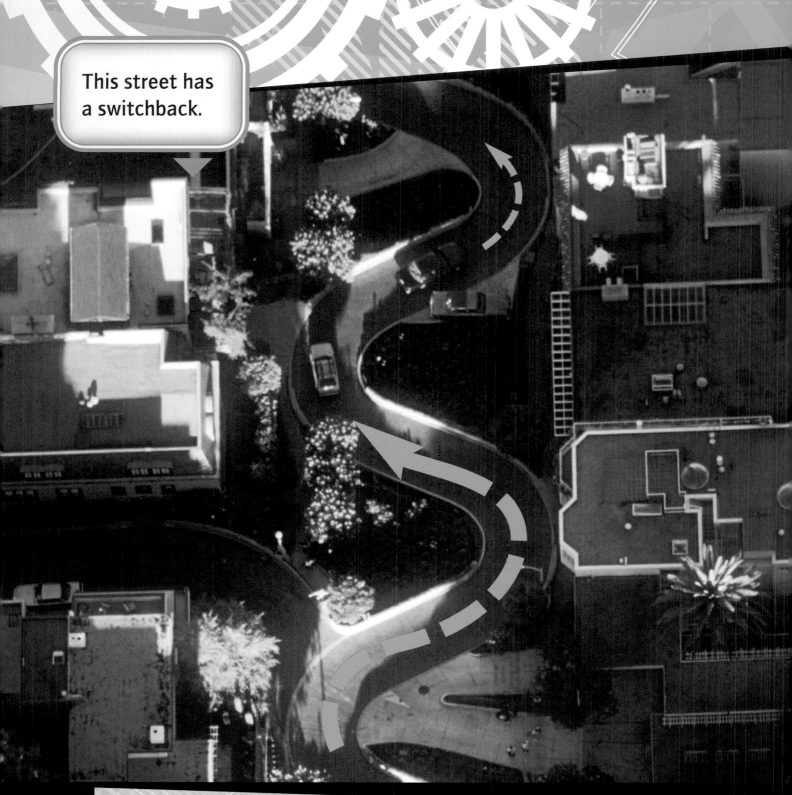

This street has a switchback.

Lombard Street in California is a winding road. One block has eight switchbacks!

Runaway Truck!

Head out to the slide at the park with a friend. Pretend a ball is a truck going too fast along a mountain road. You will need:

ball

a piece of posterboard   **slide**

Climb to the top of a slide with your ball.

Have your friend place the posterboard on an opposite angle at the end of the slide to make a runaway truck ramp.

16

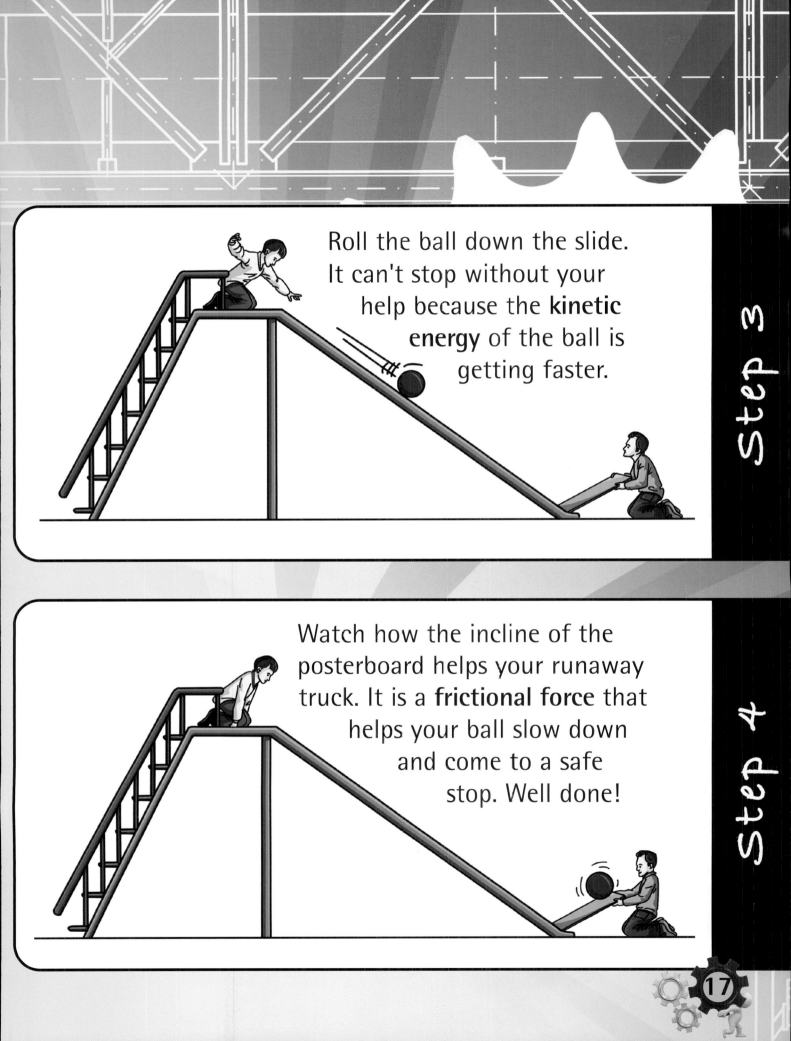

Roll the ball down the slide. It can't stop without your help because the **kinetic energy** of the ball is getting faster.

Watch how the incline of the posterboard helps your runaway truck. It is a **frictional force** that helps your ball slow down and come to a safe stop. Well done!

Chutes and Slides

Chutes and slides are inclined planes that use **gravity**. Gravity is Earth's way of pulling things down from a high place to a low place.

Chutes and slides can be flat or **convex**, which means rounded. They can be made out of materials such as plastic or metal. A slide can be rough or smooth to add or take away friction.

Construction workers use chutes to send trash to the ground.

Early Romans used chutes called aqueducts to bring water from the far hills to Rome.

Olympians go very fast on their luges, or sleds, down mountainside slides and chutes. Athletes can reach speeds of 90 miles per hour (145 km/h).

Moving Water

Let's play with curved and flat chutes to move water and discover which way is easiest. You will need:

2 paper towel tubes

a few books

scissors

foil

empty bowl

mug

Step 1

Cut the first tube in half and make it flat by putting it under a pile of books. Cover the tube with foil. Make sure the foil is not too wrinkled. If the foil is smooth, there will be less friction.

Step 2

Raise the chute to an incline. Put the bowl at the bottom of the chute. Pour water down the chute.

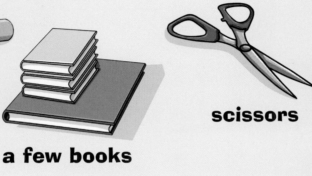

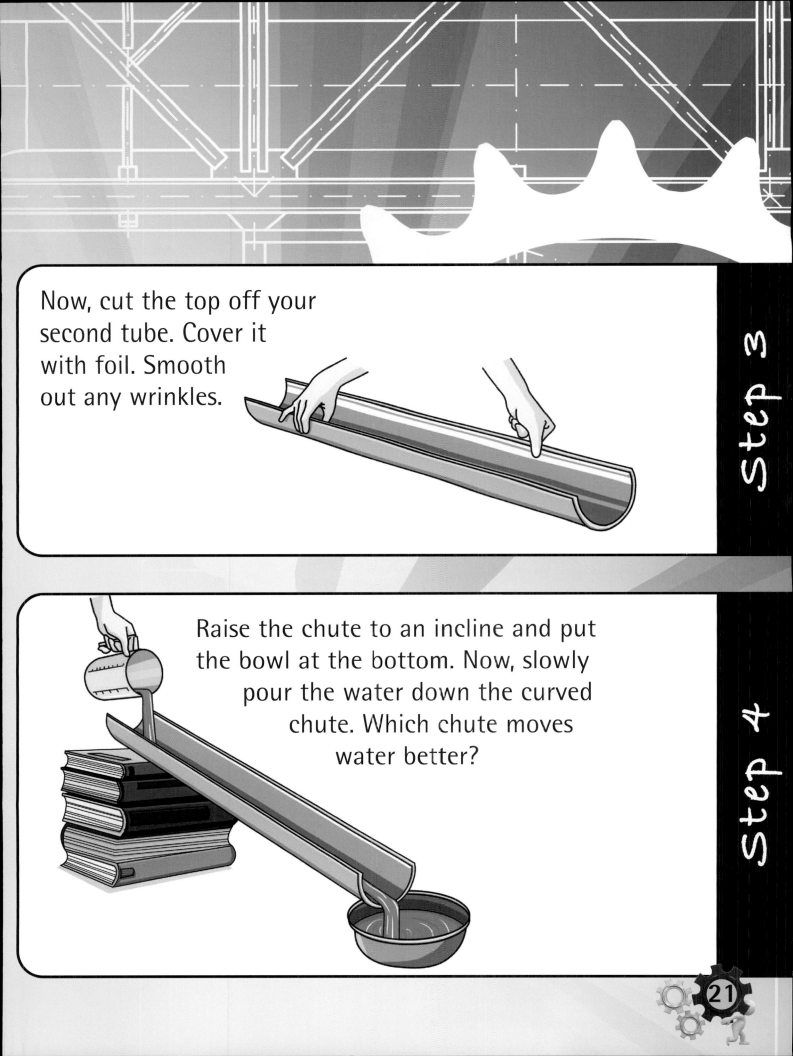

Now, cut the top off your second tube. Cover it with foil. Smooth out any wrinkles.

Raise the chute to an incline and put the bowl at the bottom. Now, slowly pour the water down the curved chute. Which chute moves water better?

Funnels

Funnels are inclined planes that often move liquid from large bottles to small bottles.

Shaped like ice-cream cones, funnels are wide at the top and have a small tube at the bottom. The drain under your sink is a funnel that takes water outside.

Pouring this liquid from one bottle to the other would be a messy job without a funnel!

Steam made by a moving ship goes through these funnels.

The silk strings near the funnel shake when dinner comes near.

Hungry Funnel-web spiders invite tired insects to land on their web's wide opening while they are hiding inside the funnel pipe!

Fill 'er Up!

Race a friend to see who can fill an empty half-gallon (2-liter) bottle with water. You will need:

2 pitchers filled with water

funnel

2 half-gallon (2-liter) bottles

Step 1

Give yourself and a friend a pitcher with water and a half-gallon (2-liter) bottle. Give only one person the funnel.

Step 2

The person with the funnel should put it on top of his or her bottle.

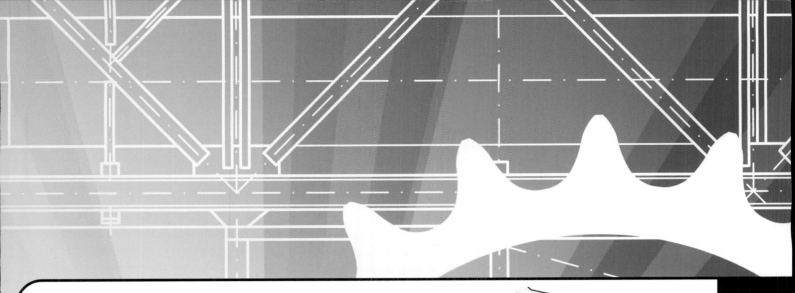

On your mark, get set, go! Start filling your bottles. Try to get all of the water in the bottle. See who fills the bottle fastest and who spills the most.

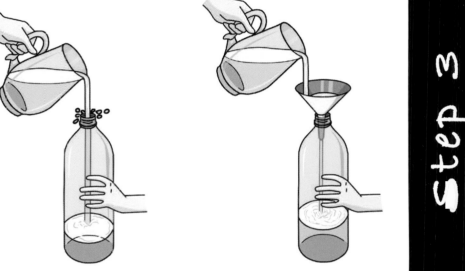

step 3

Talk about how the funnel made it easier to move the water into a bottle with a small opening.

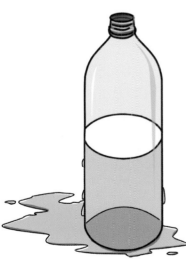

step 4

Complex Machines

Now that you have learned about several inclined planes, imagine how helpful they can be when they are put together.

When you put two or more simple machines together, a **complex machine** is made.

Funnels in this complex machine are filling bottles that are moving through a factory.

Rollercoasters are made up of many simple machines, including inclined planes, pulleys, and wheels and axles.

In Plane Sight!

Inclined planes are all around you. Go on a scavenger hunt to see how many you can find. You will need:

paper

pencil

Step 1

Find a friend.

Step 2

Look around the room you are in. Each of you should try to list as many inclined planes as you can on your paper. Number them as you go.

Move to another room or go outside. How many more inclined planes do you see? Add them to your list.

Think about what each one of these simple machines does to make work easier. Who do you think uses these inclined planes?

29

Glossary

complex machine A machine where two or more simple machines work together

convex Being rounded or curved outward

effort Force or physical energy given to a simple machine

energy The use of force to do work or move an object

flight A set of stairs between floors or landings

force Something that changes how fast an object moves

frictional force A force that slows or stops a moving object when two surfaces are pressed together

gravity The natural force from Earth that pulls things down

inclined plane A flat or level surface set at an angle

kinetic energy Energy that is made from an object in motion

mechanical advantage How much easier and faster a machine makes work

rise The height of a staircase or the distance from the top of one step to the top of the next step

steep Having a very sharp slope or incline

switchback A zig-zagged road or trail built along a steep mountain or hill

Index

Web sites

www.professorbeaker.com/plane_fact.html

teacher.scholastic.com/dirtrep/Simple/plane.htm

www.brainpop.com/technology/simplemachines

www.mikids.com/Smachines.htm

sln.fi.edu/qa97/spotlight3/spotlight3.html

weirdrichard.com/inclined.htm